To Joshua
for dancing the gypsy guitar,
photographs in striped pyjamas & all the rest

G.G.

To F.T.
for the tea, crosswords
and unwavering support

R.L.

I Miss You

Words
Gioia Guerzoni

Illustrations
Rosie Leech

Cicada Books

When we miss someone or something we love, it is very hard to keep the feeling inside. We have to express it some way so that it can turn into something different. You might miss a beautiful person, or a country you left behind, an object you used to own, or a feeling you once had. There are many things that we humans end up missing. These are little exercises to help you turn that feeling into something sweeter and easier to live with.

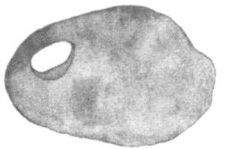

Places

When you miss someone deeply, think of a place that has meaning for both of you. Close your eyes and smell the air, sit on the ground and touch the earth with your hands. Search for a pebble that reminds you of the person you love. Spend time looking for the right one; its shape and weight should feel just right.

Think about the centuries of sun and rain and wind and history that the stone has seen. Hold onto the pebble until it becomes just another stone. Find a pond or a lake or a river or an ocean. Throw the stone in as hard as you can, so that it may continue its journey.

Lists

S pend one minute writing a list of all the things you can remember doing with the person that you miss. Simple, everyday events can make as many memories as big adventures. Write as fast as you can. When one minute is up, stick the list to a window pane so that it can be seen from outside.

Seasons

Wavy summer heat. Clouds heavy with rain. Snowflakes drifting uncertainly. Yellow leaves that refuse to part from their branches...

Wear a swimsuit in spring, a woollen cap in summer, sunglasses even if there's a snowstorm outside. Open an umbrella and feel the rain falling from the ceiling. You can do magic; you can make the sun shine brighter. Use your imagination to change the weather.

Sadness

When you miss someone, don't brush away the sadness. Instead, pull it over your shoulders like a blanket to keep you warm.

Fill glasses with tears and use them as vases for flowers. Cry in different places. Cry in private, cry in public. Cry at dawn and cry at dusk. Cry loudly, cry softly. Find the type of tears that leave you feeling empty and clean.

Animals

The word 'animal' comes from the Latin *animalis*, meaning having breath, having a soul. The poet Emily Dickinson mentioned animals and birds in hundreds of her poems. She loved them because they know but do not tell. What animal does the person you miss remind you of? Allow it to accompany you for a day. It may stay walking alongside you, or it may wander back into the wild.

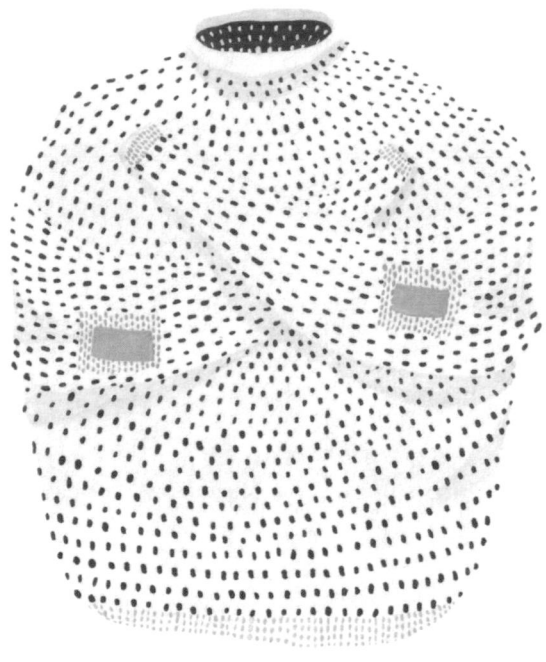

Hugs

When you can't hug someone, take their softest sweater or scarf or hat and wear it all the time. If you don't have an item of clothing, just wrap your arms around yourself and imagine that they are hugging you. Dance around the room embracing yourself.

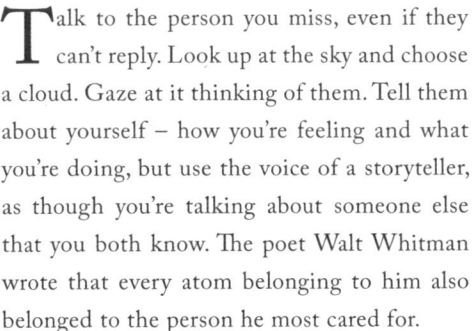

Conversations

Talk to the person you miss, even if they can't reply. Look up at the sky and choose a cloud. Gaze at it thinking of them. Tell them about yourself – how you're feeling and what you're doing, but use the voice of a storyteller, as though you're talking about someone else that you both know. The poet Walt Whitman wrote that every atom belonging to him also belonged to the person he most cared for.

When the cloud disappears or joins another cloud, the conversation is over.

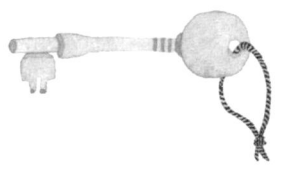

Home

The country you come from is your home. It will be your home forever, even if you have to leave it for a thousand different reasons. Think of a house with transparent walls; with a chimney and a roof, many windows and a door. Hang your paintings in the air, as the poet Pablo Neruda wrote. Your transparent home is small but you're happy in it. Imagine it in detail. You can take it with you wherever you go, like a tortoise in its shell.

Food

Taste can connect us to memories. Prepare a dish that reminds you of a person or place. Take your time cooking. Get your hands dirty; knead, bake, enjoy the smells. Taste everything at every step of the recipe.

Play music to accompany the food. The music should also evoke the person or place that you miss. Set the table for a celebration, but invite nobody. Chew in time to the music. Let the flavours and the sounds become one.

Words

Sometimes certain words become friends. And sometimes we end up in a country where we have to speak another language. If you have a special word, keep it with you like a magic charm, even if you can't translate it.

Try to boil down the thing or person that you miss, or even the feeling of missing, to a single word. It can be a real word or one that you made up. Whisper that word to yourself. Feel your lips move on each syllable like a fingerprint of sound.

Plants

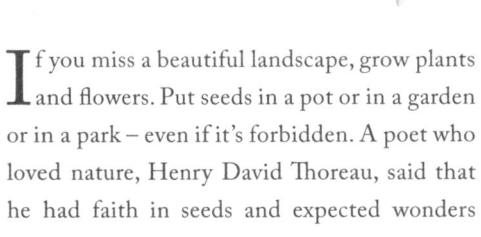

If you miss a beautiful landscape, grow plants and flowers. Put seeds in a pot or in a garden or in a park – even if it's forbidden. A poet who loved nature, Henry David Thoreau, said that he had faith in seeds and expected wonders from them.

Every day, water your flower with kindness. Free it from fears and lies as if they were weeds; help it grow and bloom. Let it remind you that even from a place of pain, transformation is always possible.

Emotions

When we miss someone or something, we feel all emotions at once. We are angry and scared and sad, even when we're also happy. Break down your feelings by spelling out the name of the person or thing you miss. Keep all the letters in your mouth. Write your sorrow with your body. Make your movements big and bold. Spell it out in anger. Spell it out in sadness. Now dance it in grace.

Letters

Write a letter to yourself from the person that you miss. Describe in detail what they are doing and what they see from their window. Feel their body on the chair, their breath as they concentrate, feel the muscles in their hand gripping the pen. Fold the letter up many times like a seed and bury it in the ground so that it can turn back into the tree it once was.

Sounds

Close your eyes and listen to the world around you. Some sounds remind us of other sounds. The roar of traffic can sound like the sea; school bells may resemble church bells; sometimes the rustle of wind in the trees seems to whisper and murmur in our ears like a voice. Other sounds are the same wherever you are, like rain on a roof, dogs barking. Compose a symphony using sounds that remind you of the person or place that you miss.

Water

Water can turn mountains into pebbles. Look at pictures of the sea and feel its vastness. Learn to make paper boats. Fill the tub and take a hot bath. If there's no tub, take a shower. Go to the swimming pool. Feel the water with different parts of your body. In summer, put your feet in a fountain; your hand under the tap. Drink it, taste it. Water has its own flavour. Water has a sound. Water cleans and also heals.

Time

Time can move differently in distant countries. In some places it moves backwards, in others it rushes forward. Have a clock in your room set to the time zone of a faraway person you miss. Look at the clock and think what they might be doing. Maybe that person is having breakfast while you have dinner, or going to sleep as you wake up. Eat dinner while they are eating dinner, even if it's early morning for you. Walk around your room at night while they are out on the street.

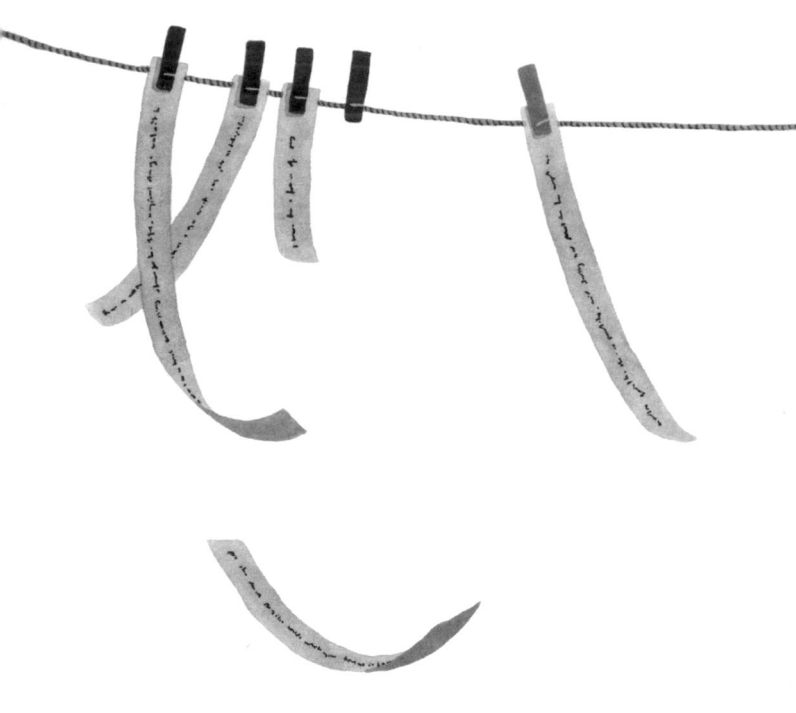

Future

Sometimes we imagine a future for ourselves that includes a person or a place, and when that person or place is gone, we can no longer imagine what the future will look like. Write down all the hopes and expectations that you have lost. Cut the sentences into long strips of paper and hang them with pegs on a string. Open the window and let the breeze move them like leaves on a branch.

Words
Gioia Guerzoni

After hopping around many countries for years, I landed by chance on a Greek island to heal a yearning heart and now I live in the middle of pistachio and pine trees in front of the sea. I have been joyfully translating literary fiction, mainly from English into Italian, for the past thirty years. I like wandering about, looking at small things, listening to languages I don't understand.

Illustrations
Rosie Leech

I studied illustration at Edinburgh College of Art. Since graduating, I have illustrated for various journals, including *Counterpoint* and *Salt & Wonder*, and have been shortlisted in the World Illustration Awards in 2020 and 2021. I collect mustard yellow garments, unruly houseplants and stories awaiting illustration. This is my first book.

Acknowledgements

Theodora Hirmes for haircuts under the trees and walks in the woods with closed eyes. Luisa Pellegrino for planting inspiration in my garden and watering it all the time. Anna Masini, Eli Gottlieb and Eileen Pun for reading this in its various forms and for the long, fun phone calls. Ziggy Hanaor and Rosie Leech for turning my scattered words into a thing of beauty. And thank you to all my other friends all over the world for being family. Miss you but getting better at it. *G.G.*

Ziggy Hanaor and Gioia Guerzoni for taking a chance on me and my tiny illustrations. Ot Pascoe for endless patience and wise advice in the face of my many questions. And, of course, my family and friends. *R.L.*

I Miss You

Text © Gioia Guerzoni
Illustrations © Rosie Leech

British Library
Cataloguing-in-Publication Data.

A CIP record for this book is available
from the British Library
ISBN: 978-1-80066-025-0

First published in 2022

Cicada Books Ltd
48 Burghley Road
London, NW5 1UE
www.cicadabooks.co.uk

Printed in China